ONE NEW HABIT
ONE BIG GOAL

**Change
Your Life
in 10 weeks**

ONE NEW HABIT ONE BIG GOAL

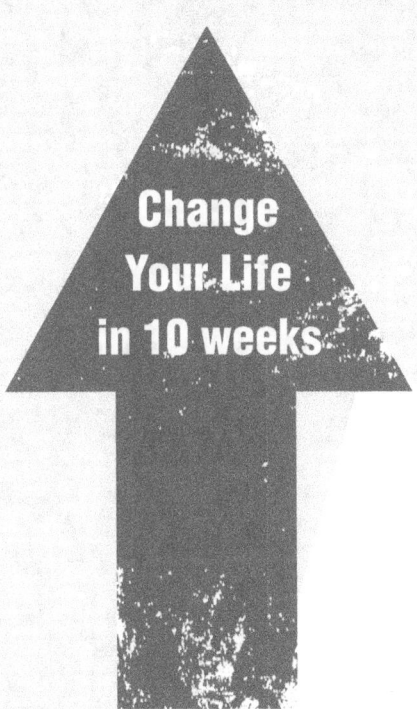

Change Your Life in 10 weeks

JACK SHITAMA

© 2018 by Charis Works, Inc.

All rights reserved. No part of this book may be reproduced in any form or by any electronic means, including information storage and retrieval systems, without permission in writing from the publisher, except by reviewers, who may quote brief passages in a review.

Published by Charis Works, Inc. in Earleville, Maryland.
Book cover and interior designed by Claire Purnell Graphic Design
Author photograph by Erin Shitama

ISBN 978-1-7320093-5-6 (Ebook)
ISBN 978-1-7320093-7-0 (Paperback)
ISBN 978-1-7320093-8-7 (Audiobook)

Table of Contents

Chapter 1 – The Myth of Self-Discipline 1

Chapter 2 – Goals and Habits 5
   Goals and Habits
   The Power of Keystone Habits
   The Power of Micro Habits
   Summary

Chapter 3 – Love the Process 13
   Thing Big, Act Small
   Progress Is Your Biggest Motivator
   Ditch Your Perfectionism
   Summary

Chapter 4 – Why You Need a Plan. 21
   Willpower and Motivation Revisited
   Accountability
   You Need a Map
   Summary

Chapter 5 – Make Your Plan 29
   Identify Your SMART Goal
   Chunk It
   Identify Your Habit
   Identify Your Bright Line
   Write Down Your Plan and Share It
   Summary

Chapter 6 – Execute Your Plan. 43
   When to Start
   Build Momentum
   Test and Learn
   Manage Your Environment
   The Dip
   Finish Strong
   Summary

Chapter 7 – Lather, Rinse, Repeat 53
   Habit Stacking and Routines
   Substitution and Insertion
   Summary

Also by
Jack Shitama

Anxious Church Anxious People

How to Lead Change in an Age of Anxiety

Introduction

I am an ordinary person. What I share in this book is for ordinary people like me. If that's you, this book can help you greatly improve your spiritual, physical and professional life. It is not complicated. The system I lay out is straightforward and easy to follow. The most important part is your willingness to focus for a short period of time: 10 weeks. Once you learn how to do this, you can continually repeat the process to become your best self.

Since this is a quick read, I suggest you read the book completely before you try to implement the system. Then go back to chapter 5 and follow each step to develop your first 10-week plan. Use chapter 6 as a resource to guide you as you execute your plan. You can get a free planning worksheet and tracking calendar at www.thenonanxiousleader.com/one-new-habit-planner.

This book is the first in a series of books designed to help leaders of congregations and nonprofits do their best work. I started with this subject because it impacts every area of life. You are more likely to be a non-anxious leader if you are spiritually and physically fit. You will accomplish more if you know how to set goals and achieve them—and this will reduce your anxiety. The simple process that I share can get you there.

Blessings to you on your journey.

Chapter 1
The Myth of Self-Discipline

"We first make our habits. Then our habits make us."
John Dryden

I am undisciplined. I've known this all my life but have tried to ignore it. When I compare myself to John Wesley, the founder of Methodism, I feel like the slacker that I am. Wesley typically arose at 4:00 a.m., began every day with prayer, and accomplished more in one day than most of us achieve in a week.

According to one account[1], Wesley traveled 5,000 miles per year by horseback and preached not less than 15 sermons per week. He journaled daily and kept a diary that marked his activities by the hour. He fasted twice a week. In between his daily routines, his travel, and his preaching, Wesley managed to write prodigiously, visit from house to house, oversee the establishment of schools and chapels, and raise funds to care for those in need.

Wesley was methodical. That's actually where the term "Methodist" came from. It was not meant originally to be a compliment. But Wesley's methodical ways were powerful.

Maybe you also believe you are undisciplined. You tell yourself that if you tried harder or had more willpower, you would grow spiritually, eat better, exercise, and accomplish more.

Here's the problem: Self-discipline is not about trying harder. The truth is, self-discipline or, more correctly, willpower, is an exhaustible resource.

A now famous experiment in 1996 by Roy Baumeister and his Case Western Reserve University colleagues demonstrates this[2]. They subjected participants to the aroma and presence of freshly baked chocolate chip cookies. Some of the participants were allowed to eat the cookies. Others were told they could not and were told to eat radishes instead (these participants were not happy).

Both sets of participants were then asked to go to another room for what seemed to be an unrelated challenge. There they were asked to solve a puzzle. What they didn't know was that the puzzle was unsolvable.

The result?

The radish-eaters made fewer attempts and spent less than half the time attempting to solve the puzzle compared to the cookie-eaters or to the control group, who had faced neither cookies nor radishes.

The conclusion of this experiment is that self-discipline, self-control and willpower are exhaustible resources. The more you use them, the less you have available. The students who had used their willpower to abstain from eating chocolate chip cookies had less willpower available to apply toward solving the puzzle.

In their book *The ONE Thing: The Surprisingly Simple Truth Behind Extraordinary Results*, Gary Keller and Jay Papasan list the factors that can deplete your willpower[3]:

- Implementing new behaviors
- Filtering distractions
- Resisting temptation
- Suppressing impulses
- Taking tests
- Trying to impress others
- Coping with fear
- Doing something you don't enjoy
- Selecting long over short-term rewards

This explains why you can't resist that quart of ice cream or bag of chips after you've had a taxing day.

The authors go further and contend that self-discipline is not something that is available at our beck and call. So if you think you are not self-disciplined, you're not alone. Sometimes we have self-discipline—when our willpower hasn't been depleted. Other times we don't.

Here's the key: People who get the results they want aren't more self-disciplined than others. What they *are* able to do is concentrate their efforts long enough to develop a positive habit. Once that habit is developed, they are able to do it without thinking and without depleting their willpower. Then they do it again to add another positive habit.

If you apply this process to your life, you will be doing amazing things without depleting much of your willpower at all. This leaves much more willpower available to deal with the many challenges that each day brings.

We can apply this process to our spiritual lives. Prayer, meditation, reading scripture, and journaling are habits that, when developed, keep us focused on what really matters. That's a must for effective leaders.

We can apply this process to our professional lives, too. Reading, writing, research, sermon preparation, planning, and learning new skills are habits that can boost our productivity tremendously.

We also can apply this process to our physical lives. Eating right, exercising, flossing, and drinking plenty of water are habits that will help us feel better, live longer, and work more effectively.

Keller and Papasan maintain that research supports the idea that it takes an average of 66 days to develop a new habit[4]. They caution against trying to develop more than one habit at a time. Focus on just one until it really becomes a habit, and it will no longer require any willpower. You'll just do it! (That would make a great slogan.) Then you can focus on a new habit.

Just imagine if you developed one new habit every 66 days. That would be five new habits a year. What if you did that for five years? That would be 25 new habits. Do you think your life would be different?

The good news is, you *can* do it! I'm proof.

The thing is, I didn't even know that I was doing this at the time. It just happened. My prayer life improved. I started exercising. And then I realized that there was a common process.

I dug into the learning behind this process and began to apply it to other areas of my life. I started several new initiatives in the ministry I serve. I started a blog. I wrote a book.

In the following pages, I will share with you what I learned. What you do with it is up to you.

Summary:

- Willpower is an exhaustible resource. Much of what you face during a day will deplete your willpower. Learn to live with this and give yourself a break.
- Self-disciplined people do not have more willpower. They just use the willpower they have to develop positive habits.
- Habits are powerful because they enable you to achieve meaningful things without using up your willpower.

Chapter 2

Goals and Habits

"There are seven days in the week and someday is not one of them."

Shaquille O'Neal

According to *U.S. News & World Report*, 80% of New Year's resolutions fail by the second week of February[5]. This is not a great success rate. Resolutions are not goals; they are wishes. A New Year's resolution typically is something like, "I'm going to go to the gym three times per week," or, "I'll no longer eat red meat," or, "I'm going to read my Bible every day."

A big problem with New Year's resolutions is they have no end date. They're "forever." And the thought of forever can be overwhelming. There's a reason 12-step programs use the mantra, "One day at a time." If you think about having to do something forever, you're almost certain to fail.

Even if you say you're going to do something for a year, that's too long. If you have ever made annual goals for your life or work, you may know what I mean. Annual goals lack a sense of urgency. You don't feel like you have to get started today because you have all year. Have you ever set an annual goal and then forgot about it? I have. That's what happens when there's no urgency.

That's why I like quarterly goals. They are not too long or too short, and they avoid the issue of having goals that last forever and are never met. A quarterly goal is long enough to achieve something significant, but it also is short enough to create urgency. And it just so happens that one quarter of a year is just slightly longer than the 66 days that Keller and Papasan say it takes to develop a habit.

My system uses 10 weeks for two reasons. First, 10 weeks is easier to visualize than 66 days. Second, this gives you three weeks between each cycle to plan the next goal. It uses the quarter system but focuses three weeks on planning and 10 weeks on execution. In this way, you can repeat this cycle four times each year.

Let's dig in. The first step is to understand the relationship between goals and habits.

Goals and Habits

A goal is a clearly defined objective that you want to reach. A habit helps you get there.

If you have worked in the corporate world, you likely know about SMART goals. This is an acronym for Specific, Measurable, Attainable, Relevant and Time-Bound.

Here's an example: Your son is getting married in two months, and you want to lose 10 pounds by the time of the wedding. Ten pounds in two months: this is specific, measurable and time-based. You know exactly what number you need to hit to achieve your goal, as well as by when you have to achieve it. It's relevant, because the impending wedding gives you extra motivation. It's attainable, since it's less than one pound per week. If it were 50 pounds in three months, that would not be attainable (and it would be unhealthy).

A habit is something you develop to help you achieve your goal. The great thing about a habit is that its effect will last well beyond your goal achievement. For example, let's say the habit you decide to develop is to eat all your meals on salad plates. This is a proven hack to easily manage portion control. Since you know that it takes about 10 weeks to develop a habit, you know that by the time the wedding arrives, you'll be used to eating meals this way. You can skip a few days and eat your meals at the rehearsal dinner and wedding reception on full-size plates. Because it has become a habit, you can easily start back up after the wedding using your salad plates.

At that point, you may decide you just need to maintain your weight. Or perhaps you will want to lose another 10 pounds. Either way, the habit of using salad plates for your entrée will be sustainable.

So a goal is something specific you want to achieve, and a habit is how you get there. You can apply this approach to any area of your life: spiritual, physical or professional. The important thing is to start with something. It's also important to understand that not all habits are the same.

The Power of Keystone Habits

Now that you understand that willpower is an exhaustible resource, as well as the relationship between goals and habits, it should be clear that establishing the right habits is the key to a productive life. Habits enable you to do things without thinking so you don't use up your willpower. You will have more energy left for self-discipline. You can turn your most important tasks into habits, enabling you to save your willpower for other important things, especially those that are hard to anticipate.

But not all habits are the same. In his book *The Power of Habit*, Charles Duhigg emphasizes the importance of "keystone habits[6]." These habits create momentum to establish other positive habits in your life. As you might guess, exercise is a keystone habit that results in improved health, eating practices, and personal productivity. According to Duhigg, a surprising keystone habit is making your bed. This keystone habit is correlated with increased well-being, higher productivity, and better budgeting skills.

It's important to note the difference between correlation and causation. A keystone habit doesn't *cause* a cascade of other positive habits. But it does create conditions that make them more likely.

In fact, it's not just that habits reduce our need for willpower. Developing keystone habits can strengthen our willpower. In landmark research, Megan Oaten and Ken Cheng asked six men and 18 women, ages 18 to 50 years old, to exercise more. They were given a free gym membership and encouraged to use it. The group did not exercise regularly at the start of the study. Their actual results were not overly impressive. For the first month, they exercised an average of once per week. By the end of two months they were up to three times per week.

Here is what's amazing. According to the researchers: "...participants also reported significant decreases in perceived stress, emotional distress, smoking, alcohol and caffeine consumption, and an increase in healthy eating, emotional control, maintenance of household chores, attendance to commitments, monitoring of spending and an improvement in study habits[7]." All this came about after just two months and a modest increase in exercise. A control group showed no such change.

Keystone habits strengthen your willpower. Even though it is an exhaustible resource, you can increase the amount you have when you start each day. So I actually lied when I said self-disciplined people don't have more willpower. Actually, they do. But they didn't start that way. They developed their capacity over time. And you can, too.

The keystone habit that changed my life was prayer.

I had always prayed, but life often got so busy that it was difficult to maintain a consistent practice. It wasn't a habit. About 10 years ago, I made a commitment to make prayer the first thing I do every day. It took a few months of doing this regularly before it became a habit. I'm not sure if it took exactly 10 weeks to become a habit. But once it did, the rest, as they say, is history.

Over the last decade, a series of habits have "cascaded" from my keystone habit of prayer. These include exercise, meditation, journaling and writing. They didn't happen all at once. I would feel led to apply my focus and effort to a particular practice. Over the course of time, that practice would become a habit. My own experience is that each time it gets a little bit easier to develop a new habit.

This process of habit formation has transformed me as a leader. I am more energetic, have a greater awareness of the need to serve others, and have more patience and perseverance. I am more grateful and less judgmental. I am more focused on what matters, and I am better able to stick to my priorities. All this started with a keystone habit.

Every person is different, so what might be a keystone habit for one might not work as well for others. Some things that tend to work well as keystone habits are prayer, meditation, exercise, tracking what you eat, and journaling. The best thing you can do is try something and see how it works.

Some people will start with a goal in mind and then try to identify the habit that will get them there. So if your goal is to lose 10 pounds, the habit you need might be recording what you eat. For others, the habit and the goal may be the same. If you want to pray 30 minutes each day, that's both a goal and a habit. If you want to get physically fit, which is not a SMART goal, then your goal will quantify your habit. A SMART goal would be to exercise three times per week, for 30 minutes each time, for 10 weeks.

Regardless of what you do, if your plan includes a keystone habit, the benefits are likely to last well beyond the first 10 weeks.

Once you identify your goal and habit, you'll want to take advantage of the power of micro-habits.

The Power of Micro-Habits

The hardest part of change is getting started. Micro-habits help make that easier. They jump-start the process by doing everything possible to help you succeed in very small increments.

In his book *The Healthy Habit Revolution*, Derek Doepker shows that the most important part of developing a habit is getting started. He advocates using micro-habits to develop momentum. A micro-habit is something so small it's almost impossible not to do it. In fact, you would likely scoff at it if somebody recommended it as your starting point.

Let's say your goal is to read the Bible for 30 minutes per day first thing in the morning. A micro-habit would be to set a goal of sitting in the easy chair where you plan to read and holding your Bible for two minutes each day for the first seven days. You don't actually have to read it–just sit there with it. You may read it if you like, but your goal is satisfied after you sit for two minutes while holding it. This sounds laughable. But after seven days you are more likely to start reading the bible for five minutes per day. Then, after another week, for 15 minutes. You get the idea.

Doepker puts it this way:

"Momentum creates motivation. Rather than trying to get yourself motivated before starting something, pick something so easy that you have no trouble getting started so that you create momentum—then the motivation will naturally follow. It may take a few days, weeks, or months to get into the groove, but eventually you'll find things become almost effortless[8]."

At this point it is helpful to understand how habits work. In *The Power of Habit*, Charles Duhigg does a great job of breaking down how habits work. According to him, a habit requires three components[9]:

- A cue
- The action (habit)
- A reward

Let's go back to the Bible reading example. Here's how it would look.

The CUE. Put your Bible by the coffeepot, so when you get your coffee in the morning you're reminded to go sit in your easy chair with your Bible. It's important to find a cue that really works. You can alter your environment to make it easier to get started. Here is a classic example: If you want to exercise in the morning, lay your workout clothes by your bed before you go to sleep. Another is to pack your gym bag and put it by the door or on the front seat of your car so you're more likely to go to the fitness club before work.

I have a friend who's developed the habit of getting up, jumping in the car, and driving about 30 minutes to the gym near her work. She works out, showers, dresses, and gets to work early. She discovered that if she puts her work clothes in the car the night before, when she ponders skipping her morning workout, it is easier to get up and go to the gym than to bring her clothes back into the house. Productivity experts call this a "hack," and it's a great one. The point is, if you can find effective hacks for your own habits, you're more likely to succeed.

The ACTION. Sit there with your Bible. (You'll eventually start reading it.) This part is pretty self-explanatory. It's whatever habit you want to start. But start with a micro-habit.

The REWARD. Ideally, you'll have the feeling of doing something positive. For many habits, the reward will be the way you feel after doing it. In other words, the habit is its own reward. This is called intrinsic motivation. However, early on you can give yourself some extrinsic motivation. Each day, after you complete your habit, allow yourself to do something you really like as a reward.

For example, you could say that you will allow yourself to check Facebook for every minute that you sit in the chair. This is OK in the short-term, but in the long-term you want to feel that 30 minutes of Bible reading will enhance your spiritual life. If the habit won't ultimately have its own reward, then you may want to think about choosing another habit.

The most important part of changing your life is getting started. Think about your big life goals. Get excited about them. Imagine how much better your life will be. But then think about a really small step that will get you moving in that direction. That's where you'll want to start.

Summary:

- Goals and habits go together. A goal is something specific you want to achieve. A habit is how you get there.

- Keystone habits have a positive effect on other areas of your life. Starting with a keystone habit will make it easier to repeat the habit formation cycle so you can continually improve your life.

- Starting is the hardest part. Use a micro-habit to overcome this obstacle, and you will be on your way.

Chapter 3
Love the Process

"Successful people do what unsuccessful people are not willing to do."

Jeff Olson
The Slight Edge: Turning Simple Disciplines into Massive Success and Happiness

Think Big, Act Small

Think about the things you could do to improve your life. Pray and meditate more regularly. Exercise. Eat better. Manage your time better. Spend more time with those who matter most. Read books that grow your mind. Focus on the things at work that will make the biggest difference.

Do you feel overwhelmed?

You know all the things you'd like to do, but you can't do them all at once. In fact, you should only work on one thing at a time to make it a habit. Then you can move on to the next. Remember, your goal should be to create four new habits a year.

I'm going to be more realistic. Knock it down to three habits a year. Your life will be transformed.

In *The ONE Thing*, Keller and Papasan write that if you want to see positive change in your life, you need to think big and act small[10].

This one little saying changed my life.

I had already established the habits of prayer, meditation, and regular exercise in my life. But I felt like there was something more that I needed to do. While on vacation I set two major goals for myself: to start a blog and to write a book. Since I was pretty good at establishing habits, I decided I would add 30 minutes of focused work to my morning routine. Since I have a day job, and I knew my willpower would be depleted in the evening, I needed to do this before I went to work. Setting a morning goal gave me the best chance for success.

It worked. In one year, I started a blog, published 28 blog posts, and wrote a 35,000-word manuscript. All this in about 30 minutes per day for an average of five days per week.

You can have big goals for your life. If you think about them and you get excited, that's great. If you think about them and get overwhelmed, then you need to break it down into smaller chunks. In fact, some people would argue you should start with the smallest of chunks. That's what micro-habits are.

This approach helps you focus more on efforts than results. And the research backs it up.

Stanford psychology professor Carol Dweck developed groundbreaking research on the growth mindset versus the fixed mindset. A fixed mindset believes that intelligence is a fixed trait. A growth mindset believes that intelligence can be trained. In essence, the brain is like a muscle in that, with training and exercise, it can grow in its capacity.

Fixed mindset people focus on performance, believing that it comes from natural ability or talent, which is fixed. If at first they don't succeed, they usually quit, believing they're just not capable. The stunning thing about Dweck's research is that smart kids who had been praised for their intelligence were more likely to have a fixed mindset; and they were more likely to give up when things got difficult.

Growth mindset people focus on effort. They believe that through hard work they can achieve competence, perhaps even mastery. They don't view mistakes as failures. They view them as learning opportunities. If at first they don't succeed, they literally try and try again. When discussing his many failed attempts to invent the light bulb, Thomas Edison famously said: "I have not failed. I've just found 10,000 ways that won't work."

That's the growth mindset. And effort trumps talent every day.

When you combine a focus on effort with small steps toward your goal, you greatly increase your chances of making progress. And progress is your biggest motivator.

Progress Is Your Biggest Motivator

I'm a big believer in vision. Without vision, you will wander aimlessly through life. Vision also creates energy and excitement. But without action, vision is just a dream.

Vision can motivate you. But without progress, you'll get discouraged and ultimately give up. Progress is your biggest motivator. In their article "The Power of Small Wins," Teresa Amabile and Steven J. Kramer share their research on workplace motivation. They write: "It turns out that ordinary scientists, marketers, programmers, and other unsung knowledge workers, whose jobs require creative productivity every day, have more in common with famous innovators than most managers realize. The workday events that ignite their emotions, fuel their motivation, and trigger their perceptions are fundamentally the same[11]."

What is it that fuels motivation? Incremental progress.

They go on to write: "Of all the things that can boost emotions, motivation, and perceptions during a workday, the single most important is making progress in meaningful work. And the more frequently people experience that sense of progress, the more likely they are to be creatively productive in the long run[12]."

This research applies to creativity among knowledge workers. But this progress principle applies to any meaningful endeavor. Making progress toward your goal, toward developing a habit, creates a positive feedback loop. Not only will you be getting closer to your goal, but the progress itself will motivate you. You will get excited that things are actually happening. This will make you more likely to keep going.

This is why micro-habits are so important. When you are just beginning, the most important way to jump-start your effort is to make progress. And the thing that will stop you dead in your tracks is procrastination. The more you procrastinate, the harder it is to get started. And the worse you will feel.

Conversely, incremental progress, small wins, will get you going. This is essential when you are beginning. Ideally, over time, you will learn to love the process of making progress. And progress multiplies exponentially. The more progress you make, the more motivation you have, and the more momentum you develop. This leads to greater progress and greater results. It's the domino theory.

A domino can knock over another domino that is 1.5 times larger than itself. Find the YouTube video "Domino Chain Reaction" by Stephen Morris, PhD. He starts with a domino that is only five millimeters high and one millimeter thick. This is smaller than a Tic Tac breath mint. He then lines up 12 additional dominoes that are successively 1.5 times larger. The last domino is three feet tall and weighs 100 pounds. He knocks over the first domino, which results in all the dominoes falling. A chain reaction started by a domino the size of a Tic Tac ultimately results in knocking down one that is the size of a very large dog.

Morris calculates that if he had another 16 dominoes, for a total of 29, the last would be as tall as the Empire State Building. This is the power of incremental progress. When you combine a love for the process with thinking big and acting small, you can achieve great things.

Even so, learning to love the process is more important than achieving your goals. Things won't always work out the way you plan. We'll cover how to deal with that in chapter 6. Loving the process of making progress will give you that growth mindset. It will help you to focus more on effort than results. And when you do have those small wins, it will keep you going. It's a positive feedback loop that can keep you going for the rest of your life. All you need to do is get started.

And the biggest obstacle to getting started is perfectionism.

Ditch Your Perfectionism

You can't learn to love the process if you never get started. If you are a perfectionist, you fight obstacles that others don't. Here are two.

First is the fear of failure. Perfectionists tend to procrastinate because they fear they won't succeed. This goes hand in hand with the fixed mindset. Instead of worrying about failure, you should focus on testing and learning. That's the growth mindset. Instead of thinking, "I'll never achieve my goal," think, "I'm going to get started and see what I learn."

Second is the need to be perfectly prepared. This is another form of procrastination. Let's say you set a goal to exercise 30 minutes, three times per week, for 10 weeks at your local gym. You don't want to waste money so you don't want to buy that gym membership until you're ready to go. And you won't be ready to go until you have the right workout clothes. And you need to decide how many sets of workout clothes you should have so you don't have to do laundry all the time. And should you workout before or after work? Oh, and what about a gym bag? Should you get one that has a built-in charger so you can keep your phone charged? You get the point.

Perfectionists tend to want every detail planned out before committing. This leads to decision paralysis, which is just another form of procrastination. Set a start date and buy the gym membership. The rest are just details. If you are a perfectionist, you will get over it. You'll find it's not so bad not having everything perfectly planned out. You'll also find that getting started relieves you of all the worry I just described, because you'll be focused on making progress.

Once started, perfectionists, and many others, also face the sunk cost fallacy. This is the idea that once you have something invested, your "sunk costs," then you don't want to change anything. For example, you might refuse to sell a losing investment because you have too much money tied up in it, and you want to see if you can recover it. But what you have invested is gone. Your decision should be made on the future value of the investment, not on your sunk costs. (So if you're still holding on to your Blockbuster stock, you might want to sell it—if you still can.)

The sunk cost fallacy also applies to emotional investments. For example, you've been watching an awful movie for an hour. The hour of your time is your sunk cost. You think because you've already invested that amount of time, you should finish watching the movie. That's the sunk cost fallacy. Instead of watching the rest of the movie, you should ask, "What could I do with the next hour of my time that would be more fruitful or entertaining?" Find your answer, and ditch the movie.

Here are other examples of the sunk cost fallacy. You continue to eat a restaurant meal, even though you are full, because you paid for it. You continue your pursuit of a particular degree because you have put in too many years to change. You continue a bad friendship because you've known each other so long.

How does this apply to loving the process? When you are working toward your goal, you need to be able to make adjustments if things are not working. One of my students had set a goal of exercising six days per week before work. She did really well for a few weeks. But she started to realize after a few weeks that by Saturday she was exhausted. Instead of keeping her goal, which would have made her more likely to fail, she decided to make weekends optional. She was able to keep the momentum developed by her progress, but she also felt new energy from knowing things were working better.

Here is another example. I decided to try intermittent fasting. This is a technique where you limit your caloric intake to a certain time period so that your body can "fast" for a period of at least 12 hours. For example, you only eat between 12:00 and 8:00 p.m. This means your body fasts overnight and through the next morning for a total of 16 hours. Intermittent fasting is a way to reduce insulin levels and burn fat without reducing your caloric intake or changing what you eat. You just change when you eat.

So I tried it, and I set a 10-week goal. What I found was that I started to get headaches after about 12 hours of fasting. I tried increasing my water consumption. I reduced my caffeine. Nothing I did worked. But I wasn't surprised. Having a headache has always been one of the telltale signs that I am hungry.

After about eight weeks I stopped. I had no doubt I could have finished the 10 weeks and developed a habit. The eight weeks were a sunk cost. I couldn't get them back, but I decided another two weeks of headaches was not worth reaching my goal.

The good news: I was focused on the process. I didn't feel like it was wasted time. I enjoyed trying it out and learning more about myself. Even though I "failed," I feel like I'm now even more in tune with my body and its rhythms. I love this process of trying things, learning, adjusting and pivoting. Or, if necessary, stopping altogether. To me, this is a lifelong process of getting a little better each day. And I love the process. You can, too.

Summary

- Think big, act small. It's great to have big goals for your life, but start with a very small step.

- Focus on incremental progress. Small wins will keep you motivated.

- Perfectionism feeds procrastination, so don't let it hold you back. Perfect is the enemy of done.

Chapter 4
Why You Need a Plan

"If you fail to plan, you are planning to fail."
Benjamin Franklin

I am not the best planner. I'm a Perceiver (P) in the Myers Briggs Type Inventory (MBTI). A P is someone who likes to go with the flow. They don't like to get boxed into a particular course of action without any flexibility. I had a clergy colleague say to me that she was a P and that's why she could never finish her sermons. I couldn't believe it! I can never finish my sermons either. I will get all the way to where the ending should be, but I will go into the pulpit without one, just so I can go with the flow. You might say this is so I can let the Holy Spirit direct me. But it is actually more because, as a P, I just can't commit in advance to a specific ending.

The opposite of a P in the MBTI is a Judger (J). This is a bit misleading, because a J is not judgmental. A J likes lists with specific things to check off as they're completed. A J likes closure and certainty. A J loves a plan. If you're a J, you probably don't need to be convinced that you need a plan. You want one.

This chapter can still help you understand how valuable a plan is.

If you're a P, then this chapter is a must. When we're talking about changing your life, setting goals, and establishing habits, your chances of succeeding without a plan are almost nil.

I'm a runner. I didn't start out that way. I decided I needed to get some exercise. We had a treadmill that I hadn't been using. I got into the habit of walking and reading on it every morning. I didn't have a plan. It just happened. I think it was a mid-life crisis. Regardless, it's better to be lucky than good.

After a few months, when it was already a habit, I got bored with walking and started running on the treadmill. After a few months of this, I got bored with the treadmill and tried running in my neighborhood. I was hooked. The irony of all this was that I had hated running before this. I played sports growing up, and running was the worst part for me. But somehow I became a runner.

This was in the fall. The following spring I entered a 5K race. I did OK, but I decided I needed to train for the next one. There was a local race that was coming up, and I found a five-week training plan. That's when I became convinced of the value of a plan. Each day had a specific workout and goal based on my desired finish time. I followed it religiously and ran what is still my best 5K time ever (I'm not getting any younger).

That's what a plan does. It can take an idea, a goal, a dream, and make it into reality.

Let's break it down.

Willpower and Motivation Revisited

As you now know, willpower is a limited resource. Good habits can help us build our capacity for that resource. And the best way to develop a good habit is with a good plan.

A good plan conserves your willpower because it reduces the amount of effort used in decision-making. As I mentioned, the 5K plan had a specific activity and goal for each day of the week. Five of those days were runs of various lengths. Each had a target time. So the goal for those days was laid out in a way that minimized the amount of thinking I had to do. The other two days of the week were rest days. Those were a slam dunk.

Since I had gotten into the habit of running in the morning, the training plan reduced the amount of friction that might prevent me from running. I went to bed the night before knowing exactly what my distance and time goals were. I don't remember if I actually did every workout, as this was quite a few years ago. Life can get in the way sometimes. I do know I must have done enough of the workouts to get positive results. I also don't remember if I hit the time goal every workout. I'm guessing I didn't. What I do know is I became a believer in the power of a good plan.

My next goal was a half-marathon the following fall. I found a 13-week training plan, and I followed it faithfully. That's different than "exactly." I did my best to do the prescribed workouts, but I'm sure I didn't do them all, nor did I hit all the goals. But it worked. I completed my first half-marathon.

For someone with no self-discipline and an aversion to plans, this was like a miracle. But I learned that a good plan greatly reduced the amount of willpower required to work toward my goals. I also learned that a good plan gave me motivation. As I noted in the last chapter, there is power in small wins. There is a flywheel effect to incremental progress. Like a flywheel, it develops momentum that makes it harder to stop. A plan not only increases your likelihood of putting in the daily effort, but the progress that you make along the way will also be a huge source of motivation. There is a positive feedback loop that multiplies motivation.

When I train, I use an app on my smartphone that records my run in real time. What I learned from my first few training plans was that I could look at my results over time. I noticed two things. One, I was logging regular training runs that were increasing my fitness and moving me toward my race goal. Two, my times for specific workouts were getting incrementally better. They weren't getting spectacularly better; just incrementally. But that was enough to keep me motivated.

A good plan, combined with regular feedback, is an enormous source of motivation. This highlights the importance of feedback to keeping motivated.

Here's an example: How motivated are you to drive the speed limit in any given situation? Of course, the answers to this question will vary. Some people want to be safe. Others want to arrive sooner. Still others want to avoid a speeding ticket. (Well, we *all* want to avoid a speeding ticket.)

Do you know the best way to reduce speeding? It's not a speed trap. And it's not higher fines. It's radar speed signs.

You've probably seen a radar speed sign. It's an electronic sign that will flash your speed at you as you approach. The newer versions will flash your speed if you're over the limit and will flash "Thank You" if you're under. Multiple studies have shown that this is the most effective way to reduce speeding. It also shows the power of feedback. When you are driving, you're getting an instant reading as to whether you're speeding or not. And most of us will slow down without even thinking when the sign flashes that we're over the speed limit.

If you have a plan and you measure your progress, you will be more motivated. Even if you're not perfect, which you likely will not be, the fact that you are measuring your incremental results will increase the chances that you will stick to your plan and will see positive results.

Of course, there also is the possibility that you won't like your results and will lose motivation. We'll deal with that in the execution phase.

For now, realize that a good plan will reduce the amount of willpower needed and will increase your motivation to succeed. When you combine that with accountability, you have a recipe for success.

Accountability

John Wesley said: "Support without accountability promotes moral weakness. Accountability without support is a form of cruelty." To succeed in life you need both. There's no such thing as the self-made person. This is critical when applied to setting goals and developing habits.

In a study by Dr. Gail Matthews, 267 participants from businesses and organizations representing six countries were asked to take different approaches to goal setting and achievement. Only 149 people completed the study. This shows how few people follow through with their goals, even when they are part of a formal research project.

The approaches ranged from just thinking about goals all the way to writing them down, formulating action commitments, sharing their goals with a friend, and sending weekly progress reports to that same friend. Matthews found that those who wrote down their goals were 42% more likely to achieve them.

This is what Matthews wrote in the conclusion section (the bold print is from Matthews):[13]

1. **The positive effect of accountability was supported.** Those who sent weekly progress reports to a friend accomplished significantly more than those who had unwritten goals, wrote their goals, formulated action commitments, or sent those action commitments to a friend.

2. **There was support for the role of public commitment.** Those who sent their commitments to a friend accomplished significantly more than those who wrote action commitments or who did not write their goals.

3. **The positive effect of written goals was supported.** Those who wrote their goals accomplished significantly more than those who did not write their goals.

This research demonstrates that once you develop your plan, you need to write it down. Neuroscience backs up Dr. Matthews' research.

Neuropsychologists have shown that we have better memories of those things that we generate ourselves. They call this the generation effect. By developing your own goal and plan, it becomes a greater part of your consciousness. Further, writing down your plan facilitates a process called encoding. This is how information is sent to the brain's hippocampus, which plays an important role in consolidating it from short-term to long-term memory. Writing your plan improves its chances of being encoded in your long-term memory.

Finally, thinking about your goal and plan uses the right hemisphere of your brain, which is the imaginative center. Writing it down engages your left hemisphere, which is the logical, analytical side. Writing it down engages your entire brain in a way that makes it a part of both your conscious and subconscious mind. This will improve the way you think about it, approach it, and execute it.

Having a plan and not writing it down is better than having no plan at all. But writing it down will burn it into your memory and make it more likely that you will succeed. Sharing that plan with a friend further increases the likelihood of success. Holding yourself accountable to that friend through weekly progress reports gives you the best chance to succeed.

You Need a Map

Driving today is different than in the old days. I used to get out a map, find my destination, and decide the route that I was going to take to get there. GPS is different. You plug in the address, and it gives you the directions one turn at a time.

Because of this, how you get there does not become part of your consciousness. I have a niece who worked in a clothing store not too far from her house. This was before every smartphone had a GPS app, and you actually had to have a separate unit in your car. Her father was on vacation with us and happened to take the GPS out of the car for the trip. He got a call from her asking how to get to work. She had been working there for a year, and because she used GPS, she never actually learned how to get there.

That brings up another difference between GPS and a map. Even if you know how to get somewhere, you are likely to use GPS in case it needs to reroute you around a bad accident or construction slowdown. So you never plan in advance how you will get somewhere. You let the GPS do it for you. You put in the starting and ending points, and the GPS does the rest. It gives you each step, and it determines that step based on the existing conditions. With a map, you decide how you will get there. Plus, you (not the GPS) will have to decide what adjustments to make if you encounter problems along the way.

With a map, you are the one that makes the decisions. You decide the starting point, the destination, and your route. You decide what adjustments you need to make. That's what a plan does for you when you are trying to reach an important goal or develop a positive habit. Without it, you will be like my niece where the path is not seared into your consciousness. You know that you want to get somewhere, but you are flying by the seat of your pants to get there. When you're trying to reach an important goal, there is nobody who is going to prompt you with the step-by-step path.

Your plan is your map. You know your starting point. It gives you a clear idea of your destination, and it lays out all the steps you need to take to get there. You might need to reroute yourself along the way. But you are much more likely to get there if you have a map.

Now that you know that you need a plan, the next step is to put one together.

Summary:

- A plan reduces the amount of willpower required to work toward your goal.

- A plan gives you a way to measure your progress, and progress is your biggest motivator.

- A written plan increases the likelihood that you will achieve your goal by 42%.

Chapter 5
Make Your Plan

Making your plan is the most important step toward changing your life for the better. The good news is, it doesn't have to be a long, drawn-out procedure. And you don't have to write a book (I'm doing that for you!). What you do need to do is put some thought into a few key steps. Let's get started.

Identify Your SMART Goal

We touched briefly on SMART goals in chapter 2. Let's dig in to the details to help you come up with a meaningful goal. Remember that a SMART goal is specific, measurable, attainable, relevant, and time-bound.

Specific

This is the heart of your goal. Expressed properly, it will give you a precise target to shoot for. It will also create energy and motivation.

Ask yourself: What would I like to achieve, and why does it matter to me? Rather than thinking about something achievable, think about something that excites you. Yes, of course you want an achievable goal. But you're more likely to pour yourself into the effort and to love the process if the goal excites you.

For example, don't just say, "I want to lose weight." Say, "I want to fit into a size 10 evening gown." Especially if you want to wear it at your son's wedding. Don't say, "I want to start running." Say, "I want to complete my first 5K." Don't say, "I want to pray regularly." Say, "I want to pray daily."

Depending on what part of your life you feel most led to improve, different goals will create different amounts of motivation. Choose the one that gets you most excited. And be specific about it.

Measurable

This goes hand in hand with being specific. In fact, it's not likely to be specific if it's not measurable. But you can also add depth to the goal. You can say that you're going to lose 10 pounds so you can fit into a size 10 dress. Or that you will complete the 5K after 12 weeks of training and run it in less than 30 minutes. Or that after 12 weeks you will be praying for 30 minutes each day.

Regardless of what you decide, think in terms of weight, time, output, frequency or completion (either you did it or you didn't do it).

Attainable

Not only must you choose an attainable goal, but it also has to be realistic; within your available time, resources and energy. You might want to fit into a size 10 dress, but if you have to lose 50 pounds in three months to get there, that's not realistic or healthy. Training for a 5K that's three months away may be realistic. However, if you've never run regularly, then training for a marathon that's three months out may be more than you can realistically achieve. Praying for 30 minutes every morning might be attainable. But if you have three school-age kids and you have to leave for work at 6:30 a.m., it might not be—unless you're willing to get up every morning at 4:30. You may not always know if your goal is realistic when you first write it down. As you execute your plan, you will get a better feel for whether you can put the time and energy into achieving it.

There is a sweet spot for this part of it. If your goal is unrealistic you'll know in the back of your mind that you really don't have a chance. This will demotivate you. On the other hand, if you make your goal too easy you'll also be less motivated.

Think of your starting point and your end point as connected by a rubber band. If your goal is too far from where you are now, the rubber band will have too much tension and will snap. If your goal is too close to where you are now there will be no tension at all. Ideally you want to set a goal that is achievable but is a stretch. With the right amount of tension your goal will pull you toward its achievement.

Relevant

Nothing occurs in a vacuum. Your goal has some connection to your life. Making the connection explicit will increase your chances of success. It will also help you determine if achieving your goal really moves you toward your bigger life objectives. A good question to ask is, "Why do I want to achieve this goal?" Maybe you are training for a 5K so you can develop an exercise habit to improve your health—or so you can look better. Maybe you just want to say you completed a race. Each of these reasons is valid.

Nobody can tell you why you want to achieve your goal. Only you can do this. But it's important to think it through. Whatever your reasons, identifying them makes your goal more meaningful, and this will increase your motivation.

Time-Bound

This is pretty straightforward. By when will you achieve your goal?

I want you to think in terms of 10 to 12 weeks. Remember that 10 weeks is the average amount of time it takes to develop a habit, and 12 weeks is an ideal timeframe to allow you to achieve something significant while still maintaining a sense of urgency.

If your vision for your life includes some really big goals—which it should—then determine what you can achieve in the first 10 to 12 weeks that will really move you toward those goals. Remember, this is an iterative process. You will set your first goal and work toward it, developing a new habit along the way. Then you'll set the next. And the next. Over time you will be a person who continually improves in all aspects of your life. And you'll love the process.

When I did some deep thinking and planning a few years ago, I knew that I wanted to write a book about leadership. I also knew that this wasn't where I needed to start. I decided that the way to get started was to start a blog on leadership. The first step was to actually launch the blog. Once that goal was achieved, I knew I wanted to be able to post articles regularly. The hardest thing for bloggers is to develop content on a regular basis. So that was my next quarterly goal. Once I had achieved that and felt confident I could write regularly, I was able to start thinking about writing a book.

The time-bound element of your goal should be whatever you can achieve in 10 to 12 weeks that will move your life forward. Don't worry that it might not be enough progress. This is a marathon, not a sprint. Four or five goals per year may not sound like much. But it's probably more than you've achieved up until now. That was certainly the case for me.

Now that you have your SMART goal, it's time to map out your plan to get there.

Chunk It

Chunking is the process of breaking down your goal into bite-sized chunks. For example, if you had a goal to read the entire Bible in a year, you would need to read four chapters a day each and every day. Of course, as I just mentioned, we are focused on a quarterly effort, so in this case you might take the first quarter of the Bible, set that as your end goal, and then read four chapters a day to hit that goal. The great part about this is that after the first 12 weeks you will have a lot of momentum toward your annual goal. You can divide your plan into chunks, by task, by time, by total, or some combination of the three.

Task

Chunking by task is standard procedure in project management. The simplest approach is to sit down with a piece of paper and write down every task you can imagine that will be required to get to your goal. Don't worry about putting them in order or about forgetting something. The idea is to get as much as possible out of your head and onto paper before you start organizing. If you miss something, that will become clear as you lay out your plan.

For example, if your task is to write a book, then you can start writing down the different steps involved. It can be as simple as developing an outline, doing research, and writing the manuscript. Once you have these written down, you might break each of those individual tasks into smaller chunks. You might do research one day and outline a chapter the next day. You could repeat the process until you have your outline completed and you're ready to write. The important point is to have a task defined for each day that you plan to move toward your goal.

I will note that you don't have to define a task to do seven days a week. In fact, if you say that you're going to work on your goal five days per week, you can schedule a week in advance, giving yourself some room for unforeseen circumstances. That way if you miss a day you can still make it up. It's not realistic to say you're going to do something seven days a week (except perhaps eat). That is a recipe for making yourself feel bad when you inevitably aren't able to follow your plan.

If you are a person who likes lists and closure, then task-oriented chunking will make you happy. It will allow you to see all the steps at once and will give you the satisfaction of checking those off as you go along.

Time

This approach breaks movement toward your goal into time blocks. For example, you can work toward your goal 30 minutes a day, five days a week. In total, you will spend two and a half hours each week on achieving your goal. Dividing this amount of time into 30-minute chunks is much more achievable than completing one two and a half hour time block. Also, over time you will develop momentum as you continue to make incremental progress. Remember: Incremental progress is one of your biggest motivators.

This approach is not so concerned with the specific tasks on which you'll be working. Instead, it lays out your plan in terms of the amount of time you will commit. If you are a Myers-Briggs P, you will likely prefer this approach to task chunking. Why? Because you are not locked into specific tasks. You just know that you are going to do something to move closer to your goal.

Using the example of writing a book, you would plan to work on it in 30-minute time blocks. One day you might do research, and another day you might focus on outlining. You may even decide you want to get started on your manuscript before you fully complete the outline for your book. Regardless, you will make continual progress in 30-minute increments toward achieving your goal.

Total

This approach to chunking works in terms of output. Instead of concentrating on specific tasks or how much time you are putting into achieving your goal, you think about what you are producing to get there.

In our book example, the typical approach would be to think in terms of words written daily. If you set a goal of writing 250 words per day, five days per week, after 12 weeks you will have written 15,000 words. You will be well on your way to completing your manuscript. Double this output, and you'll have written 30,000 words.

Another example would be to measure the number of calories you eat every day. While your ultimate goal might be to lose a specific number of pounds, you would chunk your effort by limiting your caloric intake to a specified daily number. According to the Mayo Clinic, if you reduce your caloric intake by 500 calories a day, you will lose about one pound per week. Your results will vary depending on the nature of the calories and how much you are over your ideal weight. But 500 calories is a good rule of thumb. So if you need to lose 10 pounds to get into that dress, and your normal intake is 2,000 calories per day (the average for a woman), then you can lose one pound per week by limiting yourself to 1,500 calories per day. This is a simplification, but it works. And there are smartphone apps that make it very easy for you to count calories.

I should note that you are not limited to just one of these approaches to chunking. In fact, some of the best approaches combine two or all three. If you are training to run a race, you can go online and find a training plan. It will take a 12-week plan and break it down into daily increments, each day having a specific distance and time goal. It will even include your rest days for you. This type of approach uses all three. It has the task (running or rest), the time (the goal time for the activity), and the output (the distance run).

Using one or more of these approaches to chunking will help you develop a plan that will work. The key to executing the plan is building a habit to get you there.

Identify Your Habit

Habits and goals go together. Both are needed to achieve continued improvement in life. Sometimes you set the goal first. If you then identify the habit that will help you make progress toward your goal, you are more likely to achieve it. Other times you may want to develop a specific habit; then you can set a goal to help you measure your achievement. Let's look at both.

What's important about habits is they reduce the amount of willpower required to get something done. If you develop a habit to achieve a goal, when you reach that goal you can continue to apply that habit to achieve other goals. By definition, since it's a habit you will be able to maintain that habit without using any willpower.

Let's say your goal is to lose weight, and you've expressed that in terms of a finite number of pounds. There are a number of options for developing a habit to achieve that goal.

- As mentioned previously, you can count calories.
- You can develop the habit of eating your meals off of salad plates. This is a proven hack to reduce portion sizes.
- You can develop the habit of preparing your meals in advance. This ensures that you are eating a healthy diet and reduces the likelihood of eating foods that will increase your weight.

Regardless of what you choose, if you focus on developing a habit to reach your goal, once you reach your goal you will be able to continue that habit to sustain your ideal weight.

Let's go back to the example of writing a book. The habit you develop is to write regularly. Whether you measure your effort in terms of the amount of time you write daily or the number of words you produce, you will be establishing a habit that, after 10 weeks, will be automatic. Of course, you will apply that habit to completing your book. But then you can apply it to your next book. Or to starting a blog. Or to freelance writing. You set the goal, establish the habit, and, once achieved, use the habit to reach your next goal.

As I mentioned, 10 weeks is the average amount of time it takes to develop a habit. So the idea of developing a 10-week plan is that you will not only reach your goal for that time, but you also will develop a habit that will benefit you in the future. That's why if you have a big goal it's important to break it down into components that can be achieved in 10 weeks.

Conversely, your goal may be to establish a habit such as reading the Bible every day. In this case, the habit drives the goal. Your focus is to set a goal that will help you to make the habit stick.

So now you have a SMART goal, you've broken it down into manageable chunks, and you've identified the habit that will help you get there. The next thing is to establish a bright line to keep you on track.

Identify Your Bright Line

The definition of a bright line comes from the legal world. It is an unambiguous rule or standard. A bright line leaves no room for discussion. It either is or it isn't. You either did it or you didn't.

In the case of goal and habit setting, a bright line is a pre-defined decision. It clearly states what you are going to do, without ambiguity. When you're developing your plan, you want to express your habit in terms of a bright line.

You may have already done this in the chunking process. For example, if your goal is to write a book and you have determined that your chunks are either measured in terms of words written or time spent writing, then those are bright lines. If you say you are going to write 250 words a day, five times per week, you either do it or you don't. It's the same if you say you're going to write for 30 minutes a day, five times per week. There is no ambiguity as to whether you have achieved your daily goal or not.

An important thing about a bright line is that it conserves your willpower. By pre-defining the decision, you don't have to waste energy on thinking about what you're going to do or whether you should do it. Since you don't have to think about how much you will write, you can just get to it. Having a bright line makes it easier to get started and harder to procrastinate.

Here are some other examples of bright lines. In the case of losing weight, some popular approaches are:

- I will not eat sugar.
- I will not eat carbs.
- I will limit my caloric intake to 1,500 calories a day.
- I will eat my meals on salad plates.

An example of a bright line for exercising is to set the number of times and duration per week. For example, I will run three times per week for 30 minutes each time.

The runner's training plan I mentioned previously has built-in bright lines. It has a plan for each day with specific times and output. When you look at the day's plan, you don't waste willpower thinking about how far you will run or what your target time will be. It's pre-defined. For me, when I have followed a training plan and have run the distance but didn't meet the target time, I still consider that I have followed my habit for the day. I may not have hit the goal, but I went out and did it. That's how a habit is formed.

I should also mention that your bright line can change over the course of your 10-week plan. This can reflect the incremental progress that might be built into your plan. If you set a goal of meditating for 10 minutes daily, you might want to start with the micro-habit of one minute per day to build momentum. Do that for a week. Then increase that amount by one minute each week. By the end of 10 weeks, you will be meditating for 10 minutes each day. Each week your goal for daily meditation changes, but the goal is still pre-defined. It's still a bright line.

You now have the four major components of your plan:

1. A SMART goal
2. Your chunks
3. Your habit
4. Your bright lines

Now it's time to write down your plan and share it.

Write Down Your Plan and Share It

Remember that you are 42% more likely to achieve your goals if you write them down. By now, you should also be convinced that writing your plan will increase your chances of success even more. So let's get started.

Step one is to write your SMART goal as a statement of commitment. Here are some examples.

- In 10 weeks I will have established a regular practice of meditating 10 minutes each day.
- I will complete my first 5K on (insert date).
- I will lose 10 pounds in 10 weeks.

Step two is to write down your plan in terms of chunks, habits, and bright lines.

- I will start by meditating for one minute each day. I will increase that amount each week by one minute.
- I will walk for 30 minutes, four times, in week one. In weeks two through nine I will follow the couch to 5K training plan (a training plan for first time runners).
- I will limit my caloric intake to 1,500 calories per day.

Step three is to write down how you will measure progress.

- Each day that I complete my goal, I will mark an X on my 10-week tracking calendar. (I will share more about this in the next chapter.)
- I will track my calories in my nutrition app, and I will weigh myself daily, writing my weight on my 10-week tracking calendar.

That's it. You now have your plan. The amount of detail you will have depends on your goal. The most important thing is that you have made a written commitment about what you will achieve and how you will achieve it.

Now it's time to share it.

You don't need to share your plan with a lot of people. One or two people who know you well will suffice. When thinking about whom to choose, use two criteria: dependability and honesty.

First, choose someone who is dependable. The most important aspect is to have someone who is willing to check in with you at least once a week. It doesn't do much good if you have to check in with your friend. It should be the other way around. Why? Because if you have to take the initiative, you could easily let it slip—especially if you've had a bad day or two and feel sheepish about your efforts (we'll deal with that in the next chapter). When you choose a person, ask them if they are willing to have a brief phone call every week. Set a day and time. You'll use the time to go over how your week has been and to talk about the upcoming week. You can also ask your friend to email or text you on a regular basis to ask you how things are going, as often as every day. Knowing you are going to have to answer to your friend about your progress will help keep you on task toward your goal.

Second, choose someone you know will be honest with you. Remember, support and accountability go hand in hand. It's pretty likely the friend you choose will be supportive. It's less likely they will be honest. Many people are afraid of hurting someone's feelings, so they may not give you a good kick (figuratively) when you need it. You know who those people are. You also know who is not afraid to level with you. Just knowing that they will be honest means that you know you're not going to get away with lame excuses. Of course, it's not that your intent is to use lame excuses; but good intentions don't get us anywhere. An honest friend, however, will.

So choose a friend or two. Send them your plan. Ask them to hold you accountable. Ask them to commit to a once a week check-in for 10 weeks. And ask them to nudge you regularly. If you do these things, the likelihood of achieving your goal will double.

Another approach is to set up a group. This is what I do in the course I teach. We do a combination of a closed Facebook group to report successes and failures as well as to provide nudges along the way. We also do a weekly live check-in where we share how things are going. If you have friends who want to improve their lives, then you can take the journey together. You don't have to have the same goal. Each person decides their goal, habit and plan. It's the support and accountability that will help each of you succeed. You can set up your own Facebook group or use group text. You can meet weekly in person or use any number of means to meet electronically using video or conference call. My students overwhelmingly say that it is the weekly check-in that makes the biggest difference for them.

Finally, put it out there in the world. You don't have to share your goal with all your Facebook friends (though you may). But you don't want to hide it under a bushel either. Let your friends and relatives know what you are doing. This can be scary. What if you fail? How embarrassing! But if you're willing to put it out there, it will increase your chances of success. There will be a little voice that nudges you because you know that people will ask you about your progress. This can be just enough to keep you going.

I didn't take this advice when I started writing my book. I was afraid. But after I had written a few chapters, I knew that I could do it. So I started telling people. At first, I had to force myself. I didn't want it to seem like I was bragging. But people I care about were genuinely interested. And I knew they would ask me about it when I saw them next. This created another form of accountability that kept me going.

Your friends and relatives will want you to succeed. Share your goal and how you plan to get there. They will be rooting for you. And they can help to hold you accountable. This is a recipe for success.

Now you have a plan. Ideally, it is simple but clearly defined in writing, with a SMART goal, chunks, a habit, and bright lines. You have shared it with a friend or two who will provide you with support and accountability.

Now it's time to execute.

Summary:

- Chunking makes your plan seem more achievable and less overwhelming. Your plan can be broken down into chunks of task, time, total, or any combination of the three.

- If you want to develop a habit, your goal will be the way you measure success. If you want to reach a goal, your habit will be the way you achieve it.

- Your bright line reduces the amount of friction you will encounter in executing your plan.

You can download your FREE planning worksheet and tracking calendar at www.thenonanxiousleader.com/one-new-habit-planner.

Chapter 6
Execute Your Plan

"Plans are just good intentions unless they immediately degenerate into hard work."

Peter Drucker

When to Start

It's a good idea to put some thought into when you will start to execute your plan to reach your goal and develop your habit. To do this you'll want to understand the idea of temporal landmarks. A temporal landmark is a moment in time that seems to have greater significance than ordinary moments. There are two types of temporal landmarks: social and personal. A social landmark is shared by all of us. These include the beginning of a new year, new month, or new week. They also include major holidays. The beginning or end of a school year are also social landmarks.

Personal landmarks are unique to you, such as a birthday or anniversary. There might be other days related to your work life, like the day you started an important job or the day that you retired.

What is significant about temporal landmarks is that they mark a moment in time into before and after. You can use them in your planning to not only figure out the best time to start but also the best time to finish.

Let's break it down.

Researchers at the Wharton School of Business found that using a temporal landmark as a starting point for developing a new behavior increases motivation[14]. They call this the "fresh start effect." You want to balance this with the idea that you should start executing your plan as soon as possible. Don't wait too long just so you can have a temporal landmark for a starting point. Believe it or not, a Monday, which is the beginning of the week for most people, can work just as well. Or you can start on the first day of the month. Either one of these will help you to mark the end of the old you and the beginning of the new you.

At the same time, you may want to use a temporal landmark to mark the ending point of your 10-week plan. If you can have it coincide with a birthday, anniversary, or other significant personal event, that will increase your motivation as well. If nothing else, you can try to have it coincide with the end of the month. I have found that when I am trying to achieve something, if I set a deadline that is the end of the month, it increases my motivation.

Researchers have established that using a temporal landmark for your goal deadline increases motivation. In this case it gets you thinking about your better future self. You don't need to spend a lot of time on this. As I said, the most important thing is to get started. But taking just a few minutes to look at your calendar and figure out how you can start and end your 10 weeks using temporal landmarks will give you a clear sense that you're putting your old self behind you, your new self is getting better in the present, and your future self will have achieved something significant. That's motivating.

Build Momentum

The most important part of building momentum is to start well, which is why a plan that includes micro-habits, as described in chapter 2, is so important. And, as I laid out in chapter 3, progress is your biggest motivator. A plan that includes small, achievable chunks early on will help you build motivation and momentum. To do this you'll want to do two things.

First, plan out your first two weeks and put it on your calendar. We've already established the power of writing down when and where you want to accomplish something. Rather than taking each day as it comes, you can look at your schedule and anticipate potential rough spots. For example, if you're planning to develop your habit in the early morning, then a day when you have to drive two hours for an 8:00 a.m. meeting could be a problem. You don't want to wake up that morning realizing you will have to pass on your plan. Instead, make arrangements. If you're exercising three times per week, plan your schedule so it's an off day. If you're meditating in the morning, set your alarm a bit earlier. Regardless, by looking at your calendar you can determine the best days and the best approaches to execute your plan. This is critical. By doing this for the first two weeks, you'll start to develop a habit of planning out your execution.

The second thing you'll want to do is to track your progress. Having a visual reminder of how you're doing is powerful. Just ask comedian Jerry Seinfeld. Early in his career, he resolved to work on writing comic material every day. To mark his progress, he used a large wall calendar with the entire year on a single sheet. Each day that he worked on his craft, he marked that day in the calendar with a big red X. The growing chain of X's led to his mantra, "Don't break the chain." By tracking his progress visually, he gained momentum. The rest is history.

You can combine both these approaches using the 10-week calendar provided with this book. Plan out your first two weeks, then mark each day that you succeed. Don't break the chain. Continue to plan out one week at a time, writing down when, where and what you will do. Don't break the chain. Keep the calendar in a prominent place. Put it on your refrigerator, a bulletin board, or tape it by the mirror in your bathroom. It will not only serve as a reminder of your plan; seeing the X's pile up will also create satisfaction and momentum.

One last thought about momentum. When you miss a day, put it immediately behind you. Don't dwell on it. The best thing you can do is focus on the next day and double your resolve. The process of developing a habit or achieving an important goal is the result of consistent effort. One day will not make or break you—unless you let it. If you beat yourself up about missing a day, it will generate negative thinking, which will make it harder to maintain that consistent effort. On the other hand, if you get right back on track, you'll get to your goal. Ten weeks of sustained effort will develop a habit, even if you miss a day here and there. Do your best to maintain momentum, and you will see positive results.

Test and Learn

The book *Think Small: The Surprisingly Simple Way to Reach Big Goals* is written by two of the founding members of the British Behavioural Insights Team. Also known as the Nudge Unit, this group of civil servants has the task of trying to influence behavior in the public sphere for the purpose of improving life in the United Kingdom. One of their projects was to improve the experience and effectiveness of the unemployment office. Another was to increase the collection rate for back taxes. Another was to increase the number of people who register as an organ donor when they renew their vehicle registration or driver's license.

One of the hallmarks of the Nudge Unit is that they don't make assumptions about what will work. Instead they test and learn. For example, in the organ donor project, they tested eight different messages to see which was most effective. The most successful message increased organ donor registrations by 96,000 people. The least successful actually reduced the number of registrations.

The key point here is that when you start to execute your plan you will not necessarily know what works best. Rather than adhering rigidly to your plan you need to be willing to make adjustments as you go along. This will not only improve your outcomes, it will also create momentum as you determine what will work best for your plan execution. The authors put it this way:

> Many of these experiments are referred to throughout this book and each involves asking a simple question: does it work? If I change the first line of a letter to people who've failed to pay their tax on time by telling them how many other people have paid, will it result in more people paying on time? (Answer: yes.) If I send people

a message with an infrared picture attached of their home, showing how much energy they are wasting, and compare that to the same message without the infrared image, will it get more people to insulate their homes? (Answer: no, it decreases the number of people who do so, possibly because the image shows a glowing home, which some might interpret as lovely and cosy.)[15]

The idea of test and learn is that you are constantly asking the question, "Does it work?" Does laying out your exercise clothes the night before increase the likelihood that you will work out in the morning? Is putting your Bible by the easy chair a cue to sit and read in the morning? If not, try putting it by the coffee pot.

Test and learn gives you permission to adjust as you go to improve outcomes. It acknowledges that even though you have an idea of what works best, you don't know for sure. I find this to be quite freeing. It enables me to give my best effort, but it also frees me to tweak my approach to get even better.

Remember the example of my friend who puts her work clothes in her car the night before? Her plan didn't include that at the beginning. In fact, her plan didn't even include leaving the house. She had a home gym in her garage. And she was doing a pretty good job with her daily routine. But she decided to try going to a formal program at the gym near her work, just to see if it might improve her outcomes. She signed up for a 30-day free trial, which gave her the chance to decide if it was worth paying the monthly fee. It was a huge win for her.

Life is not static. Your plan is not set in stone. You know yourself better than anyone. So take time on a regular basis to think about how you are doing and decide what you can do to get better results.

Manage Your Environment

The impact of your environment is much larger than you might imagine. In 1971, United States government officials estimated 15% of active soldiers in Vietnam were heroin addicts. The government braced for a huge problem when they returned home. However, once they were out of that environment, the problem all but disappeared without intervention. Psychologists believe the primary reason was environment. Returning soldiers did not face the combination of boredom and fear that they faced in Vietnam, nor was the drug as readily available.

Think about how your environment influences your decision-making. If you're trying to cut back on refined sugar, do you want to have Twinkies and Ho Hos in the house? If you're trying to exercise, do you want to have to haul out the treadmill every morning, or would it be easier if it were already set-up? You get the point.

Doepker writes in *The Healthy Habit Revolution*, "If you have limited willpower, that willpower is best invested in setting up a positive environment rather than wasted on having to fight against a poor environment[16]."

When you start, you won't necessarily know which environmental factors will be positive and which will be negative. That's what makes this principle so important.

You can manage your environment to reduce or illuminate negative influences and to emphasize positive influences. For example, if you are trying to lose weight, get rid of all the junk food in your house. This will make it harder for you to consume extra calories. You can't eat the ice cream in the freezer if it's not there. If you are going to eat all your meals on salad plates, then put your dinner plates in a box and store them in the basement. They will still be there when you have guests over, but it will make it much harder to use them for your regular meals.

Managing your environment does three things for you.

First, it manages friction to your advantage. Reducing friction makes it easier to do what you planned to do. If you stuff your refrigerator full of healthy food, it makes eating healthy easier. Conversely, increasing friction can help prevent what you don't want to do. Storing your dinner plates in a box will have that effect.

Second, managing your environment helps you to reduce distractions so you can focus on your plan. If you are trying to write 500 words a day, then close all the programs on your laptop except your word processor. How easy is it to get distracted when you keep getting Facebook notifications, YouTube is staring you in the face, or your email client is open so you can see every email that comes in? If you are planning to meditate, will it work better if you are in a busy place where you are likely to be interrupted, or if you choose a secluded spot? These things may seem obvious, but a little time spent thinking through how you can minimize distractions and improve focus will make a huge difference.

Third, managing your environment can encourage consistency. Just like hanging out with the wrong people in the wrong places can encourage harmful behaviors, managing your environment can encourage positive behaviors. Over time those positive behaviors will become habits that result in consistent effort.

When I started blogging, I found an old writing desk and put it in the corner of a spare room in our house. My goal was to spend 30 minutes each morning working on my blog before I went to work. My routine was to sit down at the desk as soon as I finished my prayer time. After a few months (10 weeks, anyone?), sitting down at that desk was like a signal in my head to get to work. It still is.

The Dip

"The Dip" is a concept developed by author Seth Godin in his book of the same name[17]. A Dip is the place where most people give up. In anything worth doing there is likely to be a Dip.

When you first start executing your plan, you are likely to have a lot of energy, enthusiasm and motivation. And early progress helps to amplify this. But you will reach a point where the results don't seem to be improving as quickly as they did in the early phase. This is when the Dip occurs.

What Godin points out is that the Dip creates scarcity, and scarcity creates value. This is because most people aren't able to push through the Dip, and instead give up. This is true for writing a book, exercising, eating healthy, engaging in spiritual disciplines, etc. If it were easy, if there were no Dip, then everybody would do it.

By anticipating the Dip, you can prepare yourself for it. Surround yourself with people who are cheering you on. Tell them you're going to come to a point where it will get harder, and you will get discouraged. Ask them to push you when this occurs. You will have a better chance of getting through the Dip.

Once you push through the Dip and get to the other side, you find the satisfaction of having completed your goal. The results reappear. And you realize that the Dip was only temporary. The Dip is the border between failure and success. When you push through the Dip, you get to success.

One note: Godin also cautions that we need to distinguish between a Dip and a cul-de-sac, which in French means "dead end." Sometimes we are not in a Dip; we are in a cul-de-sac. At that point we just need to cut our losses. We need to ignore our sunk costs.

Remember my attempt at intermittent fasting that I shared in chapter 3? This was a cul-de-sac. I made efforts to test and learn. But ultimately I realized that I would never get over the headaches. So I stopped doing it.

Finish Strong

Now that you have made it through the Dip, the finish line is in sight. There are several things you can do to finish strong.

First, recommit to your goal. Think about why you established this goal in the first place and think about the satisfaction you will feel in achieving it.

Second, imagine celebrating once you have reached your goal. In fact, you might even plan it out. Have dinner with a friend or loved one. Announce it on Facebook. I prefer celebrations that emphasize gratitude and relationships, because none of us achieves anything important alone. While you may think about buying that size 10 dress, tangible rewards that gratify us are often fleeting.

Third, plan out your last two weeks and put them on your calendar. This will be similar to the way you started. If you've gotten out of the practice of thinking through exactly where and when you will do your work, then this is the perfect time to reestablish that.

Finally, focus on effort and not outcomes. This is something you want to be doing throughout the 10-week process, but for your final push it's even more important. This seems counterintuitive because you're getting close to your goal, and your goal is about an outcome. But if you think too much about the final result, you can lose focus on doing the work.

I have completed three marathons. Each time, the last few miles were agony. When I thought about the finish line, it seemed like it was impossibly far away. So instead I had to focus on just putting one foot in front of the other. Focusing on effort and not on the outcome got me to the finish line.

Congratulations! You've made it to your goal. You've established a new habit. Now it's time to do it again.

Summary:

- Using temporal landmarks to add significance to the beginning and end of your plan will increase your motivation.
- Plan your first and last two weeks, write them down on your calendar, and track your success.
- Test and learn. Don't be afraid to make adjustments to your plan.
- Manage your environment to reduce friction.
- Recognize the Dip and finish strong.

You can download your FREE planning worksheet and tracking calendar at www.thenonanxiousleader.com/one-new-habit-planner.

Chapter 7
Lather, Rinse, Repeat

Once you have completed the 10-week process, you should have a good feel for how to establish a goal and develop a habit. And the more you do it, the better you will get at it. The idea is to have a repeatable process that you can use over and over to improve your life.

Don't forget to celebrate completing your first 10-week plan. It's a *big* deal. Remember that this is the beginning of a lifelong process of continual self-improvement. Don't worry about your age. I was in my 50's before I figured it out. I've had people in their 70's take my "One New Habit, One Big Goal" course. It's never too late to start. Once you get started, you want to keep the process going.

I find that I get re-energized for a new cycle when I pivot to a different area of my life. If I've just completed a habit formation cycle focused on exercise, then I might turn to something related to spiritual disciplines. Or if I've just completed the cycle focused on writing, I might turn to something related to nutrition.

I think you get the point. As you think about how you will repeat the process, you must understand the power of routines.

Habit Stacking and Routines

The most effective use of repeating the habit formation cycle is to use a process called habit stacking. This is the process of stringing together a series of habits into a routine. A routine can be done any time of day, but most productivity experts say to focus first on your morning routine. Another common time that people develop routines is in the evening. If you have a day job, the morning and evening are when you have the most control over your time.

That being said, if you have a job where there are certain important things that you need to do on a regular basis, you can establish a routine for that as well. For example, if you have a deadline that's due every week, such as a progress report or a sermon, you can develop a daily routine to get the work done. Set aside a specific amount of time at the same time every day. Then for each of those days complete a specific task, such as research, outlining, or writing.

Routines come in all shapes and sizes, but the idea is that stacking productive habits together will automatically increase your effectiveness as a person and as a professional. What makes this powerful is that the easiest way to start a new habit is to trigger it with an existing habit.

My first habit was prayer. I then got in the habit of emptying my email inbox after my prayer time. Next I tacked on exercise. I did not know I was habit stacking at the time. After a while, I had a set routine. I would get up in the morning, grab my coffee, pray, get my laptop out and process email, and then get up and run. When I started blogging, I substituted working on my blog for checking email.

Substitution and Insertion

This raises the important idea of habit substitution. You can use this process to temporarily pause one habit so you can develop a new one. Recently I decided I needed to focus on strength exercises, as all I was doing was running. During the first quarter of the year I found an exercise plan, and instead of running I substituted bodyweight strength exercises. At the end of three months, strength exercises became routine for me. Now I alternate running with strength exercises so that I have a more balanced exercise routine over the course of a week.

Of course, another way that you can use habit substitution is to substitute a good habit for a bad habit. Perhaps instead of eating dessert after dinner, you could go read your Bible or take a walk.

Another way you can develop effective routines is through habit insertion. A couple years ago I came across a journaling approach called "morning pages." This is freehand writing using a stream of consciousness approach. The key elements are writing with actual pen and paper and not worrying about what you will write, but just writing. I decided I wanted to try it, so I inserted this habit between my prayer time and my writing time. It became a habit for me in no time.

I am not a habit expert. That's what makes this process so exciting to me. I'm actually a rather undisciplined procrastinator. But by the grace of God, and with a little focus and effort, I have been able to develop habits that have changed my life.

Now it's your turn.

Summary:

- Habit stacking can help you develop highly productive routines. Use an existing habit as a cue to develop a new habit in your routine.
- Use habit substitution to try something new or to replace a bad habit with a good habit.
- Use habit insertion as another way to stack your habits and build your routines.

Endnotes

1 "John Wesley Biographical Sketch," The Go Forth Alliance, accessed October 9, 2018, http://www.goforthall.org/articles/jw_bio.html.

2 Hans Villarica, "The Chocolate-and-Radish Experiment That Birthed the Modern Conception of Willpower," *The Atlantic*, April 9, 2012, https://www.theatlantic.com/health/archive/2012/04/the-chocolate-and-radish-experiment-that-birthed-the-modern-conception-of-willpower/255544/.

3 Gary Keller with Jay Papasan, *The One Thing: The Surprisingly Simple Truth Behind Extraordinary Results* (Austin: Bard Press, 2012), 70.

4 Ibid., 56-59.

5 Joseph Luciani, "Why 80 Percent of New Year's Resolutions Fail," *U.S. News & World Report*, December 29, 2015, https://health.usnews.com/health-news/blogs/eat-run/articles/2015-12-29/why-80-percent-of-new-years-resolutions-fail.

6 Charles Duhigg, *The Power of Habit: Why We Do What We Do in Life and Business* (New York: Random House. 2012), 97.

7 Megan Oaten and Ken Cheng, "Longitudinal Gains in Self-Regulation from Regular Physical Exercise," *British Journal of Health Psychology*, Volume 11, Issue 4 (December 24, 2010), 717-733.

8 Derek Doepker, *The Healthy Habit Revolution: The Step by Step Blueprint to Create Better Habits in 5 Minutes a Day* (2014), 30.

9 Duhigg, 19.

10 Keller, 39.

11 Teresa Amabile and Steven J. Kramer, "The Power of Small Wins," *Harvard Business Review* (May 2011), accessed October 9, 2018, https://hbr.org/2011/05/the-power-of-small-wins.

12 Ibid.

13 Accessed October 9, 2018, https://www.dominican.edu/academics/lae/undergraduate-programs/psych/faculty/assets-gail-matthews/researchsummary2.pdf.

14 Hengchen Dai, Katherine L. Milkman, and Jason Riis, "The Fresh Start Effect: Temporal Landmarks Motivate Aspirational Behavior," *Management Science, Vol. 60, No. 10 (October 2014)*, accessed October 9, 2018, https://www.ncbi.nlm.nih.gov/pmc/articles/PMC4839284/.

15 Owain Service and Rory Gallagher, *Think Small: The Surprisingly Simple Ways to Reach Big Goals* (London: Michael O'Mara Books Limited, 2017), 170.

16 Doepker, 49.

17 Seth Godin, *The Dip: A Little Book that Teaches You When to Quit (and When to Stick)* (New York: Penguin Group, 2007).

Thank you for reading this book. I hope you found it helpful. If so, please leave a review on the website where you purchased the book.

You can find more articles and resources about how to be a non-anxious leader at www.thenonanxiousleader.com.

Acknowledgements

Thank you to the many people who have made this book possible. Trinity McFadden, editor, and Claire Purnell, cover and interior designer, are true professionals. They take the raw materials that I provide and turn them into finished products.

I'm thankful for my Advanced Reader Team of 49 people who reviewed the book for content, formatting and typographical errors. One can never have enough eyes look at a manuscript. They made comments and suggestions that made this book better.

I'm also grateful for the students of my course, One New Habit, One Big Goal. They helped me to refine this system by sharing their results and suggestions.

I'd like to thank my family, especially my wife, Jodi. They have supported me in so many ways. Without them, this book would not be possible.

Finally, thanks to you, the reader. I hope you found this book helpful. If it makes a difference in your life, then I will have achieved my goal.

Grace and Peace,

Jack Shitama

About the Author

Jack Shitama is an ordained United Methodist minister and the founding Minister-in-Residence of the Center for Clergy Excellence in Centreville, MD. He loves to help others become their best through his writing, teaching, speaking and coaching. He is an avid runner and has completed the Baltimore Marathon three times. Jack and his wife, Jodi, have four adult children and one grandchild. They live with no kids and no pets on Maryland's Eastern Shore.

Learn more at www.thenonanxiousleader.com. Contact him at jack@christian-leaders.com.

www.ingramcontent.com/pod-product-compliance
Lightning Source LLC
Chambersburg PA
CBHW071222070526
44584CB00019B/3119